INTERNATIONAL

[R E P R E S E N T A T I V E S]

ILLUSTRATION

[T A B L E   O F   C O N T E N T S]

BERNSTEIN & ANDRIULLI, INC.
REPRESENTATIVES

60 EAST 42ND STREET
NEW YORK, NEW YORK 10165
U.S.A.

PHONE: 212/ 682-1490

FAX: 212/ 286-1890

REPRESENTATIVES

SAM BERNSTEIN
TONY ANDRIULLI
HOWARD BERNSTEIN
JUDITH MILLER
FRANCINE ROSENFELD
MOLLY BIRENBAUM
LESLIE NUSBLATT

STAFF

CRAIG HOBERMAN
NATALIE ORTIZ
HELEN GOON
GARY EVANS

DESIGNER: B. MARTIN PEDERSEN
ART DIRECTOR: RANDELL PEARSON

SPECIAL THANKS TO IRA SHAPIRO AND THE AMERICAN SHOWCASE STAFF.

(COVER) PENCIL: PETER KRAMER FOR TOSHIBA /GLOBE: CHRIS MOORE

Art, it may be said, is where you find it. □ And we found it near and far. □ From the beginning, we not only drew from the pool of talent around us, but from distant shores as well. Finding them, the great unknowns who have since become renowned, was our great adventure. Along the way, developments in communications brought everyone closer together and at the same time, allowed us to go farther afield. The concept of time and distance changed radically, which meant the artist's location became less and less important to all-important deadlines and budgets. It wasn't long before our repertoire included the work of artists living in other hemispheres and continents. We've seen them accomplish things for our clients and themselves that even they could not have envisioned. □ After so long a run as representatives of esteemed artists, we now bring together forty of the finest. Just as each of them developed a unique talent for their craft, so we have come to appreciate what sets them apart: creativity and unusual powers of interpretation, the ability to work well with people, a quick grasp of the work at hand. □ Their inclusion in this volume is a measure of our regard for them. They are simply some of the best artists we've run across. The work gives a clear idea of their expertise and far-reaching potential. Some of it charted, some of it waiting to be discovered, as we will no doubt see. □

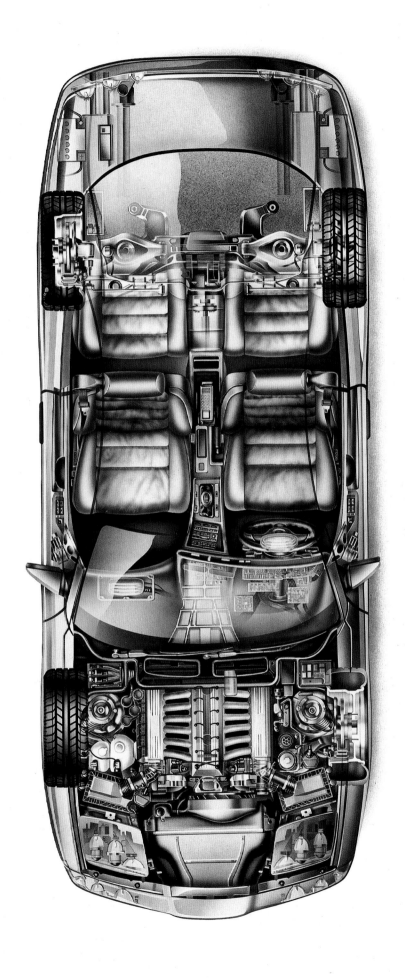

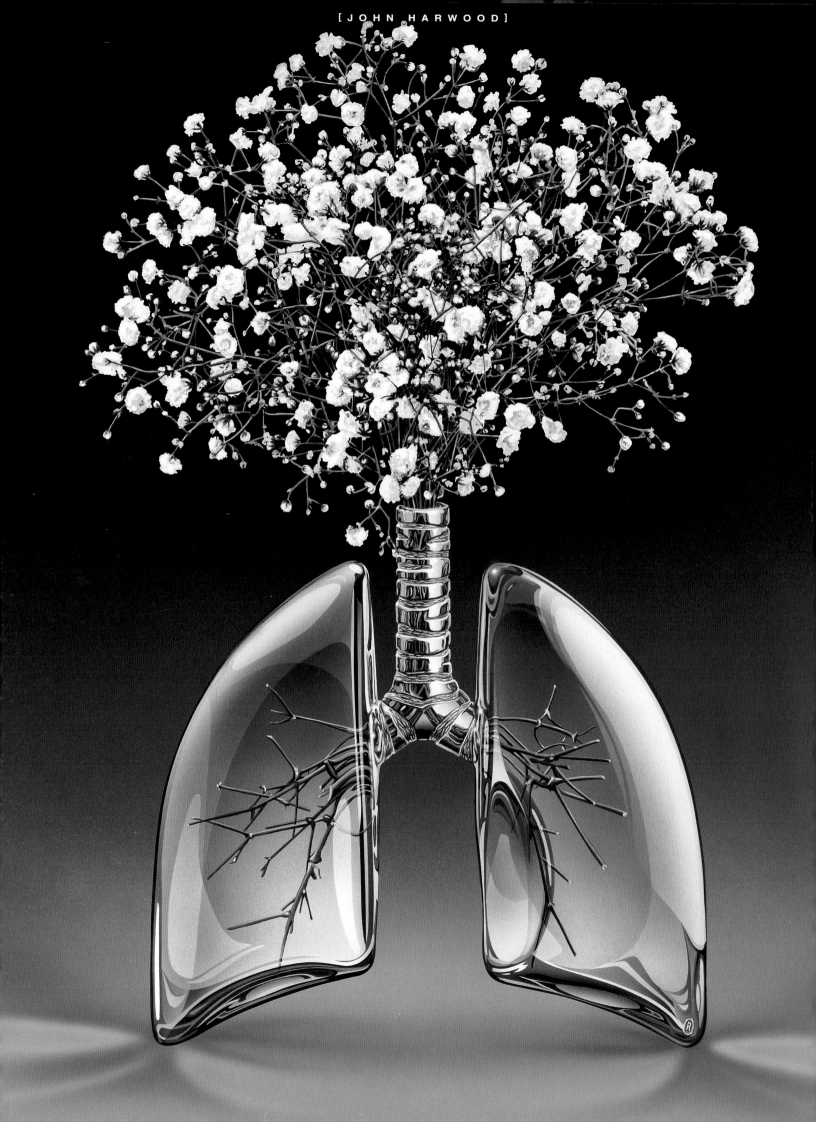

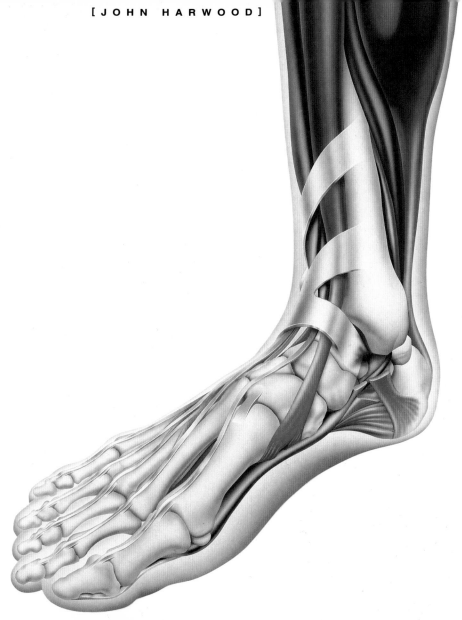

[CHRIS MOORE]

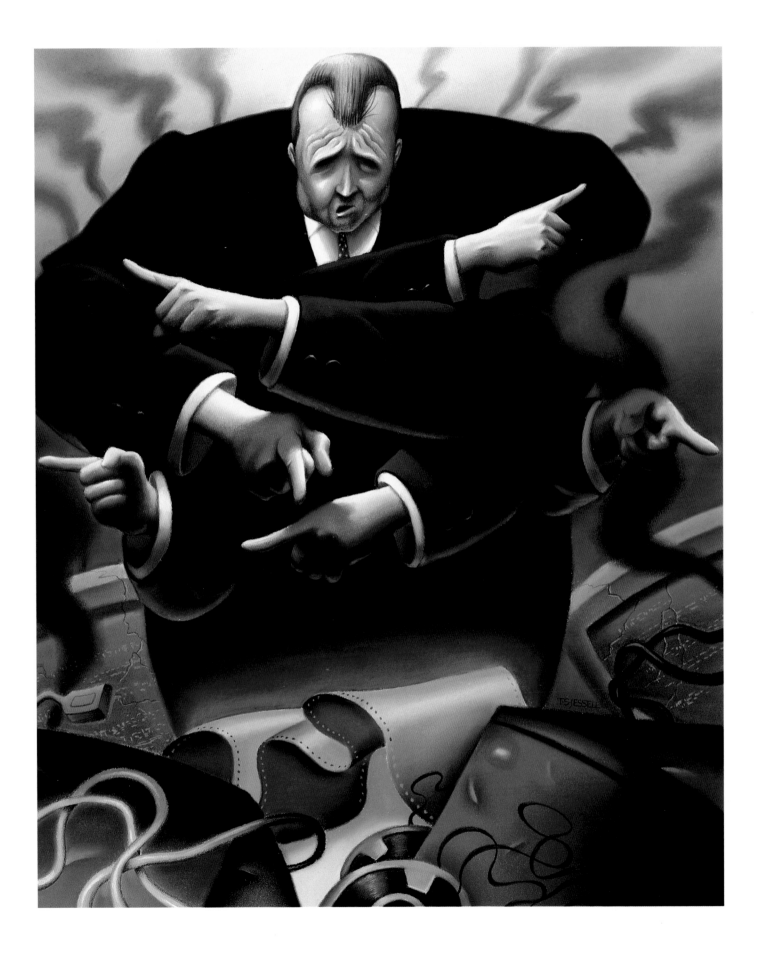

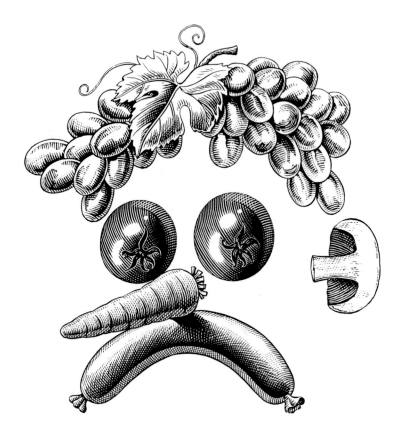

[PAM WALL]

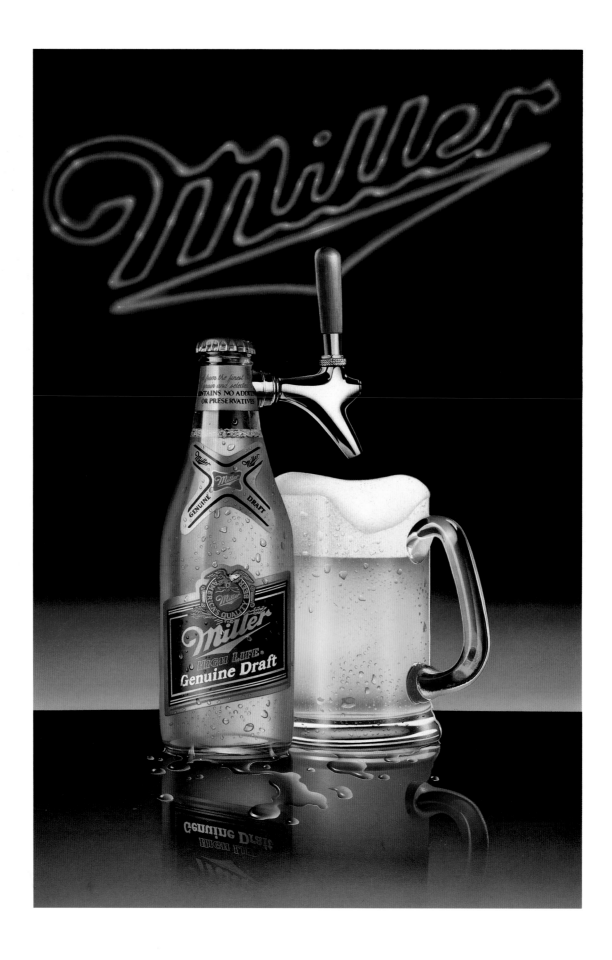

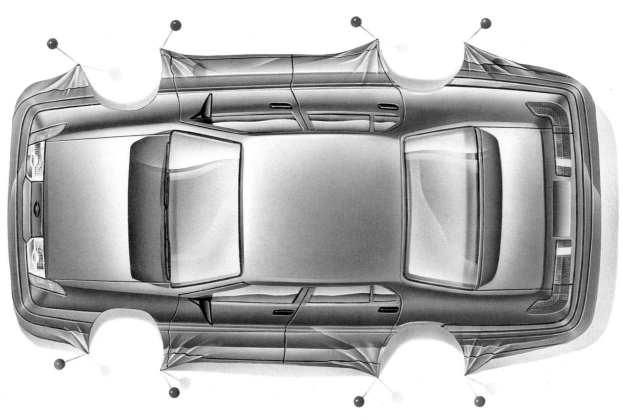

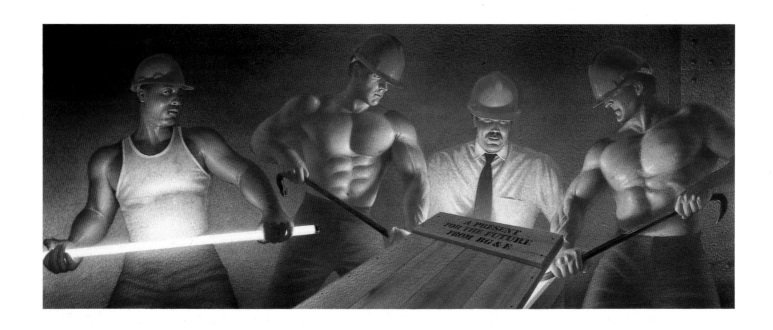

Tony Andriulli
Tony Antonios
Pat Bailey
Howard Bernstein
Sam Bernstein

David Biedrzycki
Molly Birenbaum
Rick Brown
Creative Capers
Daniel Craig

Pauline Ellison
Gary Evans
Ronald Finger
Dean Fleming
Ron Fleming

Corbert Gauthier
Joe Genova
Helen Goon
Bryan Haynes
Craig Hoberman

Tim Jessell
Hiro Kimura
Daniel Kirk
Peter Kramer
John Lawrence

Bette Levine
Todd Lockwood
Lee MacLeod
James Marsh
David McMacken

Judith Miller
Chris Moore
Pete Mueller
Craig Nelson
Jeff Nishinaka

Leslie Nusblatt
Natalie Ortiz
Greg Petan
Laura Phillips
Ray Roberts

Francine Rosenfeld
Goro Sasaki
Marla Shega
Chuck Slack
Peter Stallard

Tommy Stubbs
Thomas Szumowski
Pam Wall
Brent Watkinson
Matt Zumbo

Existing Art Library

It is quite possible that you may discover,
among the work in this book, an image that is
exactly what you are looking for. In most cases, we
can make it available to you. Immediately. In addition,
we have an extensive library of existing art. Our
research capability gives you ready access to this
fund of imagery whose scope is well represented
by the artists here. We offer it as an abiding
resource that can produce precisely what
you want to meet your objective.